A NATIONAL SYSTEM OF EDUCATION

A NATIONAL SYSTEM OF EDUCATION

BY

JOHN HOWARD WHITEHOUSE, M.P.

Cambridge

at the University Press

1913

CAMBRIDGE
UNIVERSITY PRESS

University Printing House, Cambridge CB2 8BS, United Kingdom

Cambridge University Press is part of the University of Cambridge.

It furthers the University's mission by disseminating knowledge in the pursuit of education, learning and research at the highest international levels of excellence.

www.cambridge.org
Information on this title: www.cambridge.org/9781107456044

First published 1913
First paperback edition 2014

A catalogue record for this publication is available from the British Library

ISBN 978-1-107-45604-4 Paperback

THIS book is issued with the general approval of the executive committee of the Liberal Education Group of the House of Commons though they are not necessarily committed to its detailed recommendations.

J. H. W.

4 *November* 1913.

TO

MY FRIEND

FROM YOUTH

JAMES ALFRED DALE

PROFESSOR OF EDUCATION IN

THE M^cGILL UNIVERSITY OF MONTREAL

CONTENTS

CHAPTER I

THE CO-ORDINATION OF ALL FORMS OF EDUCATION

The vital weakness of our educational system is the lack of any proper relation between primary and later forms of education. Elementary education has been regarded as a complete system in itself, capable of turning out its children at ages between 12 and 14 to enter upon the work of life. The code of the Board of Education has attempted a task at once impossible and grotesque, that of laying down a curriculum which would enable the children of the elementary schools to receive their educational equipment for life before reaching an age at which the children of wealthier parents are still in the nursery or the preparatory school. The divorce between our different classes of schools has had far-reaching results. What we have lost can perhaps best be appreciated by a reference to other countries where the whole educational system is a unity, as in parts of the German Empire, or parts of the United States of America. In these countries this has meant that when the best intellects of the day have applied themselves to the problems of education, they have been first concerned with elementary education. The phrase national education has a different meaning in these countries to that which it suggests in our country. It means a system, the basis of which is the elementary or primary school leading to all further forms of education, and these higher forms of education are intended not for children of a different social class, but for children of a higher age. In entering, therefore, upon the work of co-ordination in this country, our first duty is to cease to regard as normal or necessary the education of different social classes under different systems, unrelated save for an occasional scholarship ladder.

The basis of co-ordination of our educational system must be to regard the elementary schools as the preparatory training suitable for all normal children between certain ages, so far as their physical, mental and moral development is concerned. Secondary education in its multitude of forms would then also be regarded as the education appropriate to the varied gifts and needs of children beyond the elementary school age. Obviously a change so far sweeping in our educational ideals and machinery is a matter of gradual realization, but it will never be achieved unless the conscious ideal is before the nation and is believed in. It must, of course, first be realized by the education authorities. The private schools, whether elementary or secondary in their teaching, which are neither State supported nor managed, will, for the time, pursue their own course, but the local education authorities need only a slight extension of their powers in order to be able adequately to relate all classes of the schools founded or controlled by them. The change which is necessary in their policy can be appreciated by a reference to what is actually occurring under many education authorities in various parts of the country. The same authorities which provide elementary schools for children up to the age of 14, provide also secondary schools to which children do not naturally pass on leaving the elementary schools, but which are filled, in a considerable measure, by children who go direct to the secondary schools without having passed through the elementary school, and the ages of the children in the two classes of schools overlap.

It may be urged that whilst this is so, a considerable number of children by means of scholarships pass on to the secondary schools from the elementary schools. This is true, but the arrangement is not a scientific one. These scholarship children reach the secondary school at a later age than the other scholars of the school, and find themselves handicapped because the new school they enter has worked along different lines, and they are a year or two behind their fellow-students. The masters of the secondary schools complain, and the net result is educational loss and inefficiency. The co-ordination of the two types of schools is the only method by which this loss and inefficiency can be prevented.

The scheme of co-ordination which we press for may be very briefly summarized. Elementary education would be the form of education imposed upon pupils up to say the age of 12. About this age the scholar would pass to some form of secondary education either in the same school (as suggested in chapter III) or in a separate institution. Later he would, in many cases, be transferred to specialized forms of secondary education, as, e.g., technical institute or college, trade school, &c.

Lastly, the university would be only one of many goals to which the secondary school would lead, the boy finally going to that specialized form of education appropriate to his gifts and the work he desired to do.

This co-ordinated system might be expressed in a diagram :

ELEMENTARY EDUCATION
(for all children up to age of 12)

SECONDARY EDUCATION

University	Training College	Trade School	Art School	Technical Institute	Polytechnic	Agricultural School	Spec Insti

Attendance at many of these being accompanied with a limited amount of approved employment before reaching 18 years of age.

Any scheme of efficient co-ordination means a re-adjustment of the powers and duties of local authorities. There is no uniform system throughout the country in the matter of administrative authority. The authority for elementary education is not always the authority for secondary education. These are matters the adjustment of which requires legislation.

Such legislation must bring together the various education authorities in any area, and place upon them the duty of establishing a linked system covering both primary and intermediate education.

CHAPTER II

LEGISLATIVE REFORMS

(1) *The Raising of the School Age.*

It is scarcely necessary to-day to argue the case for the raising of the school age. There is substantial agreement, amongst all authorities, that this course is a matter of immediate necessity. The point has been exhaustively considered by the most competent Royal Commission that has sat in recent years, and the recommendations of the Royal Commission on the Poor Laws have been confirmed by a considerable number of departmental and other enquiries. There is, of course, a wide divergence of view as to the statutory provisions which should be made in this connection. However desirable it might be to enforce education up to a minimum age of 16, or even higher, it is obviously impossible to do this immediately by a simple enactment of Parliament. The local machinery has to be provided; the additional schools to be built; the qualified staff to be secured, and not least important, the money has to be raised. Obviously, therefore, whilst fixing a reasonable statutory age below which no children may leave school, the State must leave a considerable measure of responsibility and power for action to be taken after this age, to the local education authorities.   In building up a national system of education we have a special duty to guard against over-centralization.   We must trust the local authorities and encourage local initiative, and not leave all to bureaucratic control from Whitehall.

The writer suggests the immediate raising of the school age by statute to 14, and the conferring on local authorities of the power to enforce further education compulsorily for children between the ages of 14 and 18.   It is idle to hope that the latter enactment would be generally taken advantage of immediately, but it is reasonable to believe that the more enlightened municipal authorities would at once prepare to exercise their new powers, and would point the way for other authorities to follow, but a general and efficient advance on the part of the whole education authorities of the country will only come as the result of a more intelligent knowledge of and interest in education on the part of the public generally.

(2) *Control of the Education and Hours of Labour of Adolescents.*

If power is to be conferred upon the local authorities to enforce further education between the ages of 14 and 18, the State must limit the hours of adolescent labour, and the enforcement of education would be accompanied by this protection for the youth of the nation.   A practicable plan would be for the hours of adolescent labour in all districts where the education authorities put into force the new powers proposed to be conferred upon them, to be limited to four daily, between the ages of 14 and 18 ; a further period of at least four daily to be devoted to attendance at school or other educational institution. The education authorities should further have the power to enforce full time attendance at school up to the age of 16, unless the work to which the child was going, was shown to be of a beneficial and educative nature.

(3) *The Abolition of Half-time.*

One of the most melancholy features of elementary education has been the continuance of the half-timer. Condemned on physical, moral and educational grounds by every teacher and expert who has had knowledge of the system, and by every committee which has enquired into its results, it still survives, largely through the ignorance and selfishness of vested interests. The statutory raising of the school age will, of course, automatically abolish it, but Parliament and the public should be vigilant, and prevent concessions being made in this connection which would largely frustrate the object of raising the school age.

(4) *The Abolition of Juvenile Labour Outside School Hours.*

The chief Act which is concerned with the employment during out of school hours of children of school age is the Employment of Children Act, 1903. The Act gives power to local authorities to make byelaws, and it also makes certain statutory regulations affecting the labour of children. The chief employment in which children are used is that of street trading, particularly the sale of newspapers. The Act provides that no child trader shall be under the age of eleven years, but the whole spirit of the Act was regulation rather than prohibition, and the responsibility for carrying out the statutory provisions and for seeing that the regulation was adequate, was thrown upon the local authorities. In 1910 a departmental committee which was appointed by the Home Secretary to enquire into the working of the Act issued their report. It is a valuable social document. The committee find the evil of street trading to be clearly established. They describe the results of the system in grave language. They are satisfied that any form of regulation is inadequate, and they recommend statutory prohibition of street trading in the case of boys up to the age of 17, and in the case of girls up to an age not less than 18. Since the report of the committee was presented, three bills have been introduced in Parliament to carry out their recommendations. The government has now adopted a bill. The reform urged by the committee is a matter of immediate necessity. Under the present system many thousands of English children are each year having destroyed their power to become either good or healthy citizens.

(5) *The Abolition of Night Work by Young Persons.*

It is not generally realized that extensive exemptions are allowed under the provisions of the Factory Acts, by which young persons over 14 may work on night shifts in certain industries. The object of Parliament in allowing for these exemptions was to meet the needs of trades where the process of manufacture was necessarily a continuous one. The chief industry in which the system of night work for boys is most generally used is that of glass. Boys from 14 upwards work alternate weeks on night shifts for a period which varies from 8 to 12 hours at a stretch.

A departmental committee have recently enquired and reported upon the subject of all these exemptions. Their recommendations include the raising of the age under which night work is to be prohibited to a minimum of 16, though in the case of the glass works this minimum is to be attained after a period of notice.

Quite apart from the general unhealthiness and undesirability of the practice of night work for young persons, it is essential to abolish it if the further education of the young persons concerned is to be secured. We do not believe that any of the industries which use this labour are dependent upon it, or that its abolition will cause them any serious disturbance.

CHAPTER III

The Freedom of the Curriculum.

In turning to the consideration of the reforms necessary within the elementary schools, probably the first in importance is the liberation of the curriculum from the present restrictions and limitations placed upon it by existing legislation and by the code sanctioned under that legislation by the Board of Education. As we have already pointed out, elementary education has been regarded in the past as a complete scheme of education for the great majority of its scholars. The preface to the Code for the present year almost says this in terms, and the Board of Education have decided that some subjects are outside the requirements or the scope of elementary children and that these latter must be trained within certain prescribed boundaries. In actual practice this has meant that however long a scholar remains at an elementary school, say to 15 or even 16 years of age, his education has been inadequate owing to the fact that the Code does not allow of a sufficiently graduated and varied course for him. It would probably be true to say that in a great number of cases the time spent by children between the ages of 12 and 14 has been in a very considerable degree wasted. We have suggested in a former chapter that elementary education, the education suitable for children of certain ages, might appropriately end at 12 and secondary education then begin. It is not necessary to think of secondary education as a kind of education that must necessarily be given in entirely distinct and separate institutions. There is no valid reason why a secondary school should not be held in the same school in which elementary education is given, so that at the age of 12 —or perhaps a little earlier or a little later, as need might arise—children would pass from the elementary division to the secondary division. This arrangement would appear to have the following indisputable advantages :

(1) It would bring secondary education within reach of all.

(2) It would do this in the cheapest manner possible, for it would use existing buildings.

(3) This cheapness would not be at the expense of efficiency : what would happen in effect would be that the inefficient and wasteful top classes in elementary schools would be transformed into efficient secondary departments.

(4) It would tend to promote the solidarity of the teaching profession, and free circulation among secondary and elementary school teachers.

(5) It would enable great variety, both of elementary and secondary schools to be established.

(6) It would eventually break down class prejudices between the two forms of education.

The Government appear to contemplate the reversal of the Cockerton judgement which prevents higher education in elementary schools. But a warning and a protest must be entered against a visible tendency to regard this higher education in elementary schools—not as a branch of secondary education—which it must be—but as "higher elementary" education. We require no "higher" elementary schools. Such schools must have the status and freedom of secondary schools.

The Staffing of the Elementary Schools.

One evil result of the divorce between elementary and secondary education, has been the acceptance of a very different, and a lower standard, in some of the most important matters affecting the elementary school. Chief amongst these evils, is the fact that we have not made the profession sufficiently attractive to the best men and women to enter it, and a different standard to that of the secondary schools has been accepted. This has not been wholly caused by the financial difficulty. It has been in part caused also by our failure to look upon the educational system as a unity. But obviously to-day, the first necessity is to provide the means to make the profession, so far as the elementary schools are concerned, much more satisfactory and attractive. When the salaries have been raised to an adequate level; when internal reforms have been carried out within the schools themselves ; and when the Nation has ceased to view the teacher in the elementary school as occupying a less important or dignified position than his colleague in the secondary school, it will not, we hope, be utopian to believe that the men who now accept service in the secondary schools, will be equally willing to accept service in the elementary schools.

Twenty-five years ago there was a strong movement, under the direction of the late Canon Barnett, to secure a free circulation and unity amongst the teachers in secondary and elementary schools. It was thought that this could be in part achieved by establishing training colleges in connection with the universities, where men intending to enter the teaching profession would be able to take their degree and at the same time receive special training for their future work. Such training colleges were established and are now in existence at Oxford and Cambridge. They do not appear however to be much used except by men intending to teach in elementary schools, and the establishment of a free circulation between the two kinds of schools has not been realized. But the establishment of such colleges is altogether admirable, and will tend to bring to the elementary schools men equal in culture and personality to those who enter the secondary schools. The greatest of all forces in every sort of school is that of the teachers, and no amount of efficient buildings and apparatus will compensate for inadequate teaching staffs.

It is much to be hoped that the signs visible to-day of a desire for a greater unity and co-operation among the teachers in all kinds of schools will increase. It has always seemed unfortunate to the writer that so many needless artificial barriers should have been erected between different sections of the teaching profession. It is a foolish custom which has grown up of distinguishing between teachers in secondary schools and elementary schools by calling the former masters, and the latter teachers, and of speaking of headmasters in the one case, and head teachers in the other. Some local authorities have made a fine art of this practice of discrimination and, as in London, will not give either the title of head teacher or headmaster to the men in charge of their evening schools, but describe them as responsible teachers. The same tendency is seen where a local authority gives a class name, or what stands as such in the public estimation, to different kinds of schools, each of which should be regarded with the same amount of public respect. The most notable instances are where elementary schools provided by a local authority are called Council schools, while secondary schools provided by the same authority are described as County schools.

These are far from being trivial matters. In their result they affect for evil both children, teachers, and parents. It is much to be desired first that members of the staffs in different kinds of schools should have the same description applied to them, either masters or teachers, and that the heads of all schools should be similarly known by a common title, and secondly that a common official name be applied to all publicly provided and managed schools, qualified only by words signifying differences of age or specialization.

Reduction of the Size of Classes.

The reduction of the size of the classes in the elementary schools need not be argued. No one to-day opposes its desirability. The question of expense alone bars the way. But it is an improvident economy which tolerates a system under which much of its value is destroyed. This has been realized in the secondary schools, where the conditions which prevail in the elementary school are not permitted. While working for small classes all round, an immediate and very desirable instalment of the reform would be to see that in every publicly managed school there should be a small class for the older children shortly to leave school. This more intensive teaching would be of incalculable benefit to the children shortly to leave.

Art Teaching.

The teaching and practice of art in our elementary schools still remains a somewhat melancholy phase of our educational system. It is here that both the Board of Education and the highest Art Colleges and Museums have failed to give adequate guidance. Art teaching in a great number of the schools does not exist at all. In many others its limitations and the methods under which it is practised make it a grotesque waste of time. Art teaching cannot be divorced from the cultivation of the sense of beauty. It is much more than a mere exercise in drawing cubes and pots. We believe it to be an essential function of elementary education to assist in developing in every child a sense

of and a love for beauty, and the cultivation of this
sense of beauty should be a part of the art training of
the schools. It may be urged that there is no standard
of beauty, that no people agree in defining it, and that
its laws are always changing. We do not agree.
There are certain final truths on this subject which all
children should be taught. There are certain un-
changing canons of criticism which every child should
be acquainted with : simplicity in architecture ; the
suitability of buildings for their intended purpose from
the standpoint of health, utility, and the like ; colour
schemes based upon the study of nature ; the study
and appreciation of all natural forms of beauty. These
are all studies to which the child's attention should be
directed, and concerning which his intelligent sym-
pathies should be cultivated. If, as is much to be
desired, a considerable part of his education in the
future takes place out of doors, in the open air class
room or in the grounds of the school base, there will
be many more opportunities on the part of the teacher
to give fuller and better instruction on these subjects
and to develop in each child the power of cultivating
his brain by learning how to see things. In this connection an appeal should be made for a higher standard
of beauty to be observed in connection with the building and fitting up of all schools. Architecturally they
generally leave much to be desired. Internally little
taste is shown in the mural decorations. The case
for making our schoolrooms beautiful has been put
eloquently and finally by Ruskin.

"The first and most important kind of public

buildings which we are always sure to want are
schools, and I would ask you to consider very carefully whether we may not wisely introduce some great
changes in the way of school decoration. Hitherto,
as far as I know, it has either been so difficult to give
all the education we wanted to our lads, that we have
been obliged to do it, if at all, with cheap furniture
and bare walls; or else we have considered that cheap
furniture and bare walls are a proper part of the means
of education, and supposed that boys learned best
when they sat on hard forms, and had nothing but
blank plaster about and above them whereupon to
employ their spare attention; also that it was as well
they should be accustomed to rough and ugly conditions of things, partly by way of preparing them for
the hardships of life, and partly that there might be
the least possible damage done to floors and forms in
the event of their becoming, during the master's absence, the fields or instruments of battle. All this is
so far well and necessary, as it relates to the training
of country lads and the first training of boys in general.
But there certainly comes a period in the life of a well-
educated youth in which one of the principal elements
of his education is, or ought to be, to give him refinement of habits; and not only to teach him the strong
exercises of which his frame is capable, but also to
increase his bodily sensibility and refinement, and show
him such small matters as the way of handling things
properly and treating them considerately.

"Not only so; but I believe the notion of fixing
the attention by keeping the room empty is a wholly

mistaken one. I think it is just in the emptiest room
that the mind wanders most, for it gets restless, like
a bird, for want of a perch, and casts about for any
possible means of getting out and away. And even if
it be fixed by an effort on the business in hand, that
business becomes itself repulsive, more than it need
be, by the vileness of its associations; and many a
study becomes dull or painful to a boy when it is pursued on a blotted deal desk under a wall with nothing
on it but scratches and pegs, which would have been
pursued pleasantly enough in a curtained corner of his
father's library, or at the lattice window of his cottage.
Now my own belief is that the best study of all is the
most beautiful, and that a quiet glade of forest or the
nook of a lake shore are worth all the schoolrooms in
Christendom when once you are past the multiplication
table; but be that as it may, there is no question at all
but that a time ought to come in the life of a well-
trained youth when he can sit at a writing-table without
wanting to throw the inkstand at his neighbour, and
when also he will feel more capable of certain efforts
of mind with beautiful and refined forms about him
than with ugly ones. When that time comes he ought
to be advanced into the decorated schools; and this
advance ought to be one of the important and honour-
able epochs in his life[1]."

We are still far from acting on his advice. It is
not an uncommon sight in entering an elementary
school to find the main wall covered with a jumble of
incongruous charts, maps and pictures, so that we

[1] "A Joy for Ever."

have side by side a presentation portrait of the Sovereign, a diagram illustrating the action of alcohol on the human body, a tonic sol-fa notation chart and a case of bottles shewing the preparation of mustard. If there were the necessary knowledge and guidance available, it would be easy enough to make the walls of each schoolroom an education in themselves, placing before the children who were taught in them reproductions of the greatest pictures and reproductions of the most beautiful specimens of architecture and illustrations of scenes of natural beauty. This treatment would naturally lead on to an even more dignified scheme of mural paintings, under which the walls would be decorated with mural paintings fitting in with the general architectural scheme and designed to appeal, either through symbolic painting or the representation of historic scenes, or by decorative treatment of natural beauty, to many sides of the child's nature.

Manual Training.

The experience of the Montessori method has revealed the extraordinary possibilities of educating children through manual activities. The success of this scheme should lead to many experimental schools on the same lines, and it should also encourage the great extension of educational handwork in the elementary schools. The beginnings of this system are to be found in many schools already, but it has yet to receive that general recognition which is necessary.

The children of elementary schools who receive instruction in manual work usually go for an hour or

two once a week to a manual training centre. Such
an arrangement is wholly insufficient. Each school
should have its workshop, where every boy should
have training as a regular part of his work.

But apart from the workshop and the conventional
forms of manual training, we are still far from realizing
the possibilities of handwork as a help in the class-
room in nearly every subject taught. There is an
absence of synthetic treatment. If, for instance, the
children of a school could construct, in or out of doors,
under skilled guidance, a model of an old building, the
construction of the model should not be thought of as
an end in itself. Apart from the manual skill which
would be cultivated, and the actual joy to be got out
of the work itself, the whole operation should be made
the means of teaching a number of related subjects, e.g.
history, architecture, hygiene, geography.

Manual training is not to be regarded as the end
of culture but the means of culture. So far as we
possess the results of expert observation, they tend to
prove not only that handwork develops intelligence
but that it raises the level of attainment in all other
branches of instruction.

Relations between Teachers and Scholars.

As the elementary school is raised to a more dignified place in our national life, and the gulf between
their teachers and those in higher schools is diminished,
we may hope for the employment of many of the
methods common to the best secondary schools. First
among these we would place the influence to be exerted

by the teachers through establishing relations with their scholars out of school, by sharing games and outdoor activities and by establishing school clubs and societies—literary, debating, photographic, &c.—perhaps, even, by running a little school journal.

Prefects and Houses.

Closely allied are the questions of prefects and "houses." Both are features which might well be introduced into the elementary schools. The prefect system, under wise control, is capable in the elementary school of the same admirable results which have attended it in the secondary school. The house system, under which each boy would be a member of a "house" and under a housemaster who would be charged with the duty of watching over his interests during the whole of his school life, would powerfully assist the promotion of a corporate life, with all the character-making influences it means.

School Record Cards.

A development of the House system, which is recommended above, would be the institution of the school record card. These would appropriately be kept by the housemasters, and would contain a complete record of all relevant facts concerning the boy's work, progress, character and abilities. A copy of the record card would accompany the boy when he left the elementary school for some form of secondary education, and would also be at the service of the Care committee or any other authority which came into touch with the boy with the view of helping him along his life's journey. Reports, as in secondary schools, should be sent to the parents at least once a year, and parents meetings should be organized.

Teachers' Libraries.

All that enlarges the interest and outlook of the teacher should be encouraged. Much more should be done to enable him to reach the best literature dealing with educational subjects. There is sometimes a central library of educational works, but a much better system would be to supply on loan for the use of the teachers at each school copies of some of the best new books on education as they appear. Here, too, is a field for the co-operation of the libraries. In any case each teacher should have a list of all important new books, and encouraged to read them.

Rural Schools.

In surveying the whole field of elementary education perhaps no aspect of it is less satisfactory than the schools established in rural districts. It is only right that we should remember that some local authorities have made praiseworthy efforts to deal with the special problems that concern them, and in such cases gardening classes have been established and instruction given in a few simple agricultural subjects. These experiments have, however, been few in number and unduly confined in extent, and the whole system of rural education requires re-organization. It is true to say that for the most part the same unenlightened adherence to a code fixed for all kinds of schools has been shown, with the result that so far elementary education in the rural districts has not had any material, or, indeed, noticeable influence in promoting interest in the pursuits and occupations of the country, or in preventing boys from drifting as rapidly as they can to the towns and cities. There are certain reasons which should be remembered which particularly explain the lack of adequate progress in the past. These may thus be summarised :

(1) Local authorities have been hampered by the questions of finance, for, as has been already stated, the educational burden is proportionately heavier in rural districts than in large centres. This, of course, is a vital question which must be dealt with in a general national scheme of educational finance.

(2) There has been no defined and coherent elementary education policy set before local authorities in connection with the special needs of rural districts. Here we think the Board of Education should have done more. In another place we discuss the extension of the functions of the Board, and particularly of its department of special enquiries. It has an urgent work to do in connection with the rural schools of England, and it is necessary for special financial help to be given for the promotion of different types of rural schools and the encouragement of experiment generally.

In turning to the consideration of constructive proposals for the reform of rural education, we would submit the following considerations :

(a) There should be no attempt to stereotype a

curriculum and impose it on all rural schools ; the first need is for variety.

(*b*) This variety is necessary in order that the work of each rural school, both in its elementary and secondary phase, may be related to the future vocations of the scholars.

(*c*) This vocation can be roughly presumed from the character of the district and the local industries and occupations.

(*d*) The training should not only enable the scholars to follow efficiently the work they will probably enter upon when they leave school, but it should also have the wider object of enabling them to enter upon such occupations with the greater interest that springs from knowledge, and with an intelligent appreciation of the possibilities before them in county life.

It will therefore be clear that education in the rural districts should have a practical, as well as a theoretical interest. We cannot pretend in considering it to separate it into elementary and secondary divisions clearly defined, but in both divisions it should be closely related to actual experiment, and should include gardening, agriculture, the care and rearing of cattle and domestic animals, the construction of simple buildings, the principles of drainage, together with special technical and manual instruction. Part of this instruction would necessarily be given in connection with agricultural centres for specialised training, where boys from rural schools would attend on certain days in each week to supplement their school training. Experimental farms would be an essential feature of the work in connection with these centres, and smaller farms, even if they only took the form of allotments for experimental gardening, would be associated with all of the rural schools. France, Austria and other countries point the way in the use of school gardens, the former country having more than thirty thousand attached to its schools. Only in this way can we fit lads to become small-holders and interest them in taking up an agricultural career on scientific lines.

The qualifications for teachers in rural schools are not necessarily the same as for teachers in lower schools. The need for specialists has been recognized in connection with higher agricultural education and it should be possible to make arrangements by which the services of the same specialists could be available both for the secondary and the elementary school.

Part of the training in rural schools should be concerned with the business side of agricultural life, and questions of co-operation, transit, markets, and all the other points upon which the success of the little farmer or small-holder is dependent, must be made real to the students.

CHAPTER IV

THE OUTDOOR LIFE OF ELEMENTARY
SCHOOL CHILDREN

We have already emphasized the divorce between different types of schools in this country. What this means in actual working is in part seen in the different standards which exist in elementary and secondary schools for the physical care of their respective children. In the latter case there is an organized outdoor life with adequate facilities for its development. In the former these are generally absent. It is the desire of the writer to consider some methods of organizing the outdoor life of children of elementary schools. It may perhaps be found that in seeking to carry them out, something more than the physical health of the children will have been secured.

The Playground of the Elementary School.

There are some points which might first be considered which do not involve large questions of policy and expense, and could easily be dealt with. These for the most part are concerned with the school playground. It is curious how consistently this has been neglected.   It is generally reduced to the minimum amount possible, sometimes it does not exist.   It has to take the place of the playing fields invariably at the disposal of efficient secondary schools, and except in rare cases where the school is happily situated near a public park (for the problem is especially one which concerns town schools) it is the only ground available either for work or play, which is to be done outside the class room.   Notwithstanding these facts, no trouble whatever is generally taken to make the little ground that exists as useful and as efficiently planned as possible.   The school building itself, whether good or bad, is at least the result of thought and judgement ; its plans are considered and a decision is arrived at.   The school ground is the object of no such care.   It is asphalted or gravelled, surrounded by cast iron railings, and the architecture of the ground is complete.   But the playground should be as carefully considered and planned as the school itself, and even a small piece of ground, if wisely arranged, would be of incalculable good.   It should be remembered that for the town child it is both physically and mentally beneficial for as much of the school work as possible to be done in the open air.   A few tentative experiments in this direction have been tried, but the absence of proper outdoor facilities has prevented any considerable extension of them.

Outdoor Work and Class Rooms.

The outdoor class room should, therefore, be architecturally planned.   It must be considered with reference to cold, prevailing winds, privacy and other matters, sliding or movable glass partitions may have to be employed, a verandah or roof may be necessary. Obviously, therefore, in the case of a new school, all these questions must be considered in relation to the whole building. As for existing schools, all that can be done now is to plan the playground as efficiently as may be. It would then, in many cases, be possible for outdoor classes to be held daily in suitable weather. Not only would this be a great gain to the physical well-being of the children, it would promote their intellectual efficiency. A child in the open air is more alert, and capable of greater mental effort. The playground could be so arranged as to provide means whereby work hitherto done in part in the school room could be more efficiently done in the open air. Thus space should be found for at least a few small trees and plants which would not only beautify the ground, but should be used for the school work, and properly so used would provide the means whereby town boys and girls might be led to some understanding and love for the world of nature. A wise master or mistress would not be long in realizing that a London child taught day by day throughout the year to observe the living things around it, to sketch a tree in autumn and spring, summer and winter, to commit daily to paper a description or sketch of the unfolding bud, or growing leaf, would be cultivating many latent possibilities and receiving something more than bodily health.

The outdoor work of the playground need not be confined to nature study. A well planned playground would have its sand heap, not only for the play of the smaller ones, but for its educational value, the study of physical geography and the making of maps in relief.

Sometimes it may be found possible even in town playgrounds, to have miniature garden plots to be tended by the scholars and to provide simple accommodation for a few pets.

There should also be provided in the school playground the simple apparatus necessary to interest children in the study of the weather from day to day, the measurement of the rainfall and the record of temperature and wind.

Facilities for Play.

So far we have dealt chiefly with the educational value of a well planned and properly equipped playground. There remains the play side proper to be considered before we pass from this phase of the subject. To neglect its function as a playground proper would indeed be short-sighted, seeing that in the vast majority of cases unless the children can play here the only alternative for them is the gutter. The ground is, of course, always too small for the great games, football, cricket and the like, but the games which require smaller space could frequently be given facilities for. In an otherwise useless corner it might be possible to put a racquets or fives court. In building a new school the task would be made easier by so planning the building that some part of it would become available for the back wall of the court. Although it may be truly urged that not more than four persons can play at one time in games like fives or racquets, they are nevertheless of incalculable benefit in the development of a school's corporate life, and they afford the opportunity for the masters in elementary schools, by teaching their boys these games and playing them together, to promote camaraderie, and exercise that personal influence, which is the legitimate pride of the secondary schoolmaster.

Preparation of Plans and Models.

The Board of Education might well give more guidance to local education authorities on the proper planning of their school grounds.   One of the best ways to do this would be the preparation of a series of plans and models of suggested playgrounds showing the various features which might be introduced in their relation to the main buildings of the school.   These could be on view in the library of the Board of Education or elsewhere, and in other ways made available for the help and guidance of local education committees.

Holiday Use of Playgrounds.

Before leaving the subject of school playgrounds, a plea should be recorded for greater facilities being given for their use in the summer evenings and on Saturdays, and during the school holidays. The success of such use would mainly depend upon the voluntary workers who were willing to direct and share the play and hobbies of the school children. Some appeal could with confidence be made to the patriotism of the teachers who would, in the writer's opinion, come forward in increasing numbers voluntarily to share this further labour if the possibilities in it were more efficiently striven for.

Playing Fields.

Turning from the question of the playgrounds immediately around the elementary school, we have next to consider how the further needs of the scholars for adequate recreation ground is to be met. Our brief study of the question so far, though it has shown great possibilities, physical and educational, realizable through the wiser use of the ground around the school, has also made it apparent that this latter is quite inadequate to enable organized games to be shared by any considerable number of children. The playing fields proper still remain to be provided where the town child may spend long summer evenings and holidays in joyous exercise, with green grass under his feet and fresh winds blowing about him.

Ultimately this problem may be solved by the adequate planning of new towns and extensions, and the establishment of the school base which is discussed more fully in chapter VII. The immediately urgent matter is how to provide facilities for regular and organized games for the children in the existing elementary schools. There are three methods worth considering. (*a*) There should be closer co-operation with the parks' authorities with a view to more use being made of the parks, and better arrangements being made within the parks for the accommodation of the children. (*b*) The crowded parts of our cities should be roughly divided into areas and a piece of ground should be provided to be shared by all the schools within that area. Each school would use it regularly, in turn, and facilities would then exist for the holding of inter-school sports and matches, with all that these mean in promoting public spirit, as well as individual health. (*c*) The playing fields of secondary schools are frequently unused on certain days of the week, and especially at certain hours on many days. There is no good reason why with friendly co-operation between the authorities of the respective schools, the grounds should not be used during these unoccupied times by the children of the elementary schools.

The School Journey.

We turn in conclusion to consider briefly how outdoor life can be helped away from the school grounds themselves. We should like to see the school journey greatly developed in this country. One or two headmasters of elementary schools have at great personal sacrifice taken small parties of their boys on a few days tramp. Preparation has been made by the reading of appropriate books and by learning something of the history and nature of the place they were to visit. A careful scheme of work to do on the journey was prepared, provision being made for the study of science, nature, architecture. On the journey itself each boy kept a careful daily diary of all that he saw and learnt. The results in each case have been magnificent, and both boys and teachers have benefited in countless ways. The Board of Education has approved such journeys. It is for local authorities and others to give every encouragement possible for their development. Here indeed is a great field of work for the people of goodwill.

A modification of these long school journeys could more easily be put in operation. There is no reason why a party from each school should not be taken at say weekly intervals for a half-day's educational journey, visiting buildings of interest or beauty, art galleries and museums, botanical and zoological gardens, &c. The London County Council has taken a step which might well be copied by educational authorities throughout the kingdom. This is the preparation of a pamphlet containing particulars of the various institutions to which children might be taken on these educational journeys with details of the hours of opening and conditions of admission. Expeditions like these, in addition to their obvious advantages, do so much in teaching the duties of citizenship and, what is even more important, developing the capacity for citizenship.

Co-operation of the Board of Education.

The help of the Board of Education in promoting the organization of the outdoor life of elementary school children might be given in the following definite ways :

(1) By refusing to allow any weakening of the existing requirements for the size of elementary school playgrounds.

(2) By increasing the present minimum required in all cases where it is reasonably possible to do so.

(3) By giving guidance to local education committees in the more regular and systematic use of the playground for the purpose of educational work and training.

(4) By assisting the committees in the proper planning of school grounds by the preparation and loan of models and plans.

(5) By encouraging and guiding local education committees in the wiser planning and choice of sites for schools, keeping in view the desirability of establishing a school base and of using the opportunities afforded by the existence of parks.

(6) By issuing circulars or other publications dealing with long and short school journeys and setting forth the work which might suitably be undertaken on such journeys.

These suggestions for action by the Board are made because, properly conceived, it should ever be the inspiring force behind the local machinery of educational administration, guiding and creating the effort and enthusiasm which come with new ideas and methods, received with sympathy and applied with wisdom.

CHAPTER V

THE SCHOOL BASE

The isolation which exists between one form of English education and another, is in no respect more clearly shown than in the method which we continue as actively to-day as ever, of building our elementary schools in crowded and sometimes in slum areas, with inadequate ground, giving not only insufficient room for play, but causing also the erection of high buildings of several floors. The schools so built at the doors of the children for whom they are intended, will never become common schools, i.e. to be used by poor and well-to-do alike, nor can they be properly related to the higher schools in the same town or district.

We are now about to enter upon a new stage of educational organization. The proposals of the Government are being made public, and legislation must soon follow. It is, therefore, worth while to consider the question of the method followed hitherto for providing elementary schools and to see whether a healthier and more efficient, as well as a less costly method is not possible. To-day when a new school is required, either in a town or in a newly-developed suburb, the education authority generally has to buy a very costly site at

3—2

a price which prevents adequate ground being secured. The solution appears to be, so far as new districts are concerned, to take advantage of the Town Planning Act, and in adopting schemes under that Act, to make ample provision to secure adequate sites for whatever schools may be necessary in the future. But apart from town planning schemes, it should be possible for local authorities to secure and to hold in reserve whatever ground may be considered necessary for the schools of the future. I desire, however, to suggest what may prove to be a far more scientific arrangement in building both the primary and the secondary schools of the country. That is, except in exceptional cases, to cease the method of building individual schools, isolated from one another, and to establish for every small town, and for every given area of larger towns, the school base. In new districts and under town planning schemes, the establishment of the school base would be a comparatively easy matter. It would not be necessary for the base to be very far away, and it would be readily accessible for the children for whom it was intended. In the big cities, the problem of founding a school base is a much more difficult one, but it is not incapable of solution. If, for instance, it can be solved in London, no other town is likely to present greater difficulties. The immediate policy to be urged for London, is that the schools should be built in groups around certain of the great open spaces. There is, for instance, no reason why we should not gradually build around Victoria Park, or very near to it, a number of elementary schools, and these would ultimately give sufficient accommodation for a considerable portion of the surrounding district. In many cases the children would then be within walking distance of the schools; in most cases, with the assistance of train, bus or tram no child would have to walk more than a mile each way, and the child who is not in a condition to walk this distance, is not in a condition to be educated at all. What would such a scheme as this mean in the lives of the children? They would be taken to a school situated amidst country surroundings, they would exchange the crowded playground or the gutter and the noisy street for a hundred acres of grass, trees and water. Moreover, the use of the park by the school children would not interfere with its use by the general public, for during the school hours it is generally deserted, and there would be room for all.

The first, and probably the only objection to such a scheme, would be on the score of initial expense. The elementary schools for London exist, and to create a school base now would appear to mean a double capital expenditure. It must, however, be remembered that we should work towards our ideal gradually. New schools, for example, are constantly being built in East London, and there is no reason why these should not form the nucleus of the school base at Victoria Park. Gradually too, some of the existing schools could be used for infants and the younger children. Some of the present school sites are of great building value, and would probably realize a far higher price than the new sites would cost, but, of course, the scheme, even for a limited part of East London, would take years to realize. What is desirable is that an ideal should exist, a start be made. It is not unreasonable to believe that when the first group of schools had been completed at the selected base, the cost of administration and maintenance would be less proportionately than under the present system. If the base is round a public park the playground involves no cost so far as purchase is concerned. The swimming bath or pool would be shared by all the schools at the base, so too would the kitchens and dining-rooms, if it were necessary to provide a simple meal for the children at mid-day. This need not be at the expense of the public; the school canteen would be established and would supply necessary food at cost price. Necessitous children would, as now, be fed without charge. There are other features which it would appear might be shared by all the schools, with a consequent reduction of expense. These include gymnasium, the school concert room, as well as special features, like art class rooms and museums.

The proposal is also important in connection with secondary education, for there is no reason why the municipal secondary school should not be established at the school base. This would assist in building up that organic connection between primary and secondary education which it is to be hoped will be one of the chief results of new legislation on the subject of education. If it be regarded as impossible to establish the school base on a large scale, it is yet possible to adopt it within our cities in miniature form. In meeting the school needs in growing suburbs, schools could be built in groups of at least four, it being a principle that at least four times as much playground is secured as would have been available for a single school built on the old system. Sufficient ground would then be available for organized games. It would be easy to have a cricket pitch, if only matting, and football and hockey could be played.

Apart from the gain in the matter of the physical health of the children, there would be many other advantages. There would be a broader life for the children; there would be the opportunity of inter-school relations and competitions for the building up of *esprit de corps*. The system, too, would ultimately be economical for many common features could be shared by the schools, and there would be a reduction of expense in connection with cleaning and maintenance.

CHAPTER VI

THE PHYSICAL CARE OF ELEMENTARY SCHOOL CHILDREN

In another chapter we have fully discussed the arrangements for the outdoor life of elementary school children, and if those are carried out, the problem of the physical care of the children is, to a large extent, solved. The present chapter deals only with the arrangements for the physical care of the children made from inside the school, in order that the schoolroom and the playing field may efficiently co-operate. The necessary further reforms within the school may be briefly set forth in the following order :

(1) *School Clinics.*

There is to-day complete unanimity of opinion respecting the value of the medical inspection of school children sanctioned by law. The adequate treatment of school children is a necessary and an inevitable consequence. Isolated experiments deserving of all praise have been made, but the general question of treatment still remains to be faced. The most efficient, as well as the most economical, plan appears to be that of the school clinic, where doctor and dentist would attend periodically for the treatment of the children requiring it, and where physical records and measurements would be kept. The clinic would probably be unnecessary in every school, as in big centres one for a group of schools would be sufficient. When we have achieved the school base this problem like so many more would be simplified.

(2) *The Bath Room as a Class Room.*

We hope that the time is not far distant when school baths will be a feature of all elementary schools. Not only are these necessary in order to ensure the absolute cleanliness of all children in attendance, but the bathroom is necessary in order to train children not only in the habits of cleanliness but in elementary hygiene and the laws of health. The provision of such facilities would raise the whole standard of the schools, and it is far from being a question only of physical cleanliness. The fact that absolute cleanliness was enforced upon every child would do much to break down the existing prejudices of many parents against the elementary schools, and would powerfully assist the creation of the common school. Ample guidance is awaiting the educational authorities in this direction. The method of the spray baths introduced into the schools of many German municipalities leaves nothing to be desired and the results already achieved are beyond dispute.

(3)　*Organized Games.*

Organized games, both in the playground and in the playing fields and parks, which are referred to in another chapter, should form a regular and daily feature of the curriculum of the school.

In connection with the organization of play, notice should be taken of the remarkable developments which have taken place in Manchester, Birmingham and other towns, in promoting the outdoor life of the school children. In these towns a large number of people of goodwill have been brought together and have given their time and service to organizing and supervizing the play of the children in the parks and other public places. The result has been in each case most satisfactory, and the experiments have been uniformly successful. It is clear that the system could be extended generally, and requires only skilled organization united with the requisite sympathy.

(4)　*Regular Physical Training.*

In addition to organized games and play, regular and scientific physical training is necessary in all our schools, both elementary and secondary. In the latter this physical training exists in the majority of cases. It is not a difficult thing to impose it upon the whole of the elementary schools. Already the Board of Education has prepared a very full and admirable syllabus giving the necessary details of a comprehensive scheme.

(5) *Physical Records.*

The preservation of physical records should be insisted upon in all cases. These are really inseparable from any proper system of medical examination and oversight.

The goodwill of the parents is necessary in this as in so many other points affecting the schools, and it would be encouraged if each year or half year a copy of the physical record card were sent to each parent.

CHAPTER VII

THE MEANING AND SCOPE OF SECONDARY EDUCATION

We need entirely to revise our conception of secondary education. Just as elementary schools have been regarded as the schools appropriate for the children of the poor, so secondary education has been regarded as the education appropriate for the children of a higher social class. The basis upon which the whole of the suggestions contained in this book are made is the regarding of elementary education as the education appropriate for children of certain ages irrespective of their social position, and for secondary education to be regarded as continued education appropriate to a later age.

The Duty of Education Authorities.

It cannot truthfully be urged that even where education authorities have complete control of their own secondary schools, they have in many cases succeeded in building up a real relationship between the elementary and the secondary schools in their own area. The curriculum of the secondary school has usually been fixed on the understanding that pupils would begin it at an age considerably earlier than that at which they leave the elementary school. Unless, therefore, the work of the elementary school is regulated accordingly, the minority of boys who enter the secondary school from the elementary school must and do find themselves seriously handicapped. The first reform, therefore, which has to be insisted upon by the State, is the co-relation of secondary and elementary schools.

What is Secondary Education?

It is unfortunate that so awkward and meaningless a word as "secondary" has been imposed upon us to express an educational system. The lay public has attached different meanings to the word at different times, and probably the most general conception it now has of the word is that it is a description of a superior type of school. Professional opinion has, as far as possible, crystallized the meaning of the word and thinks of it as the description of a school which prepares boys for the universities, or which has a distinctly academic basis as opposed to technical schools, or schools where other than intellectual pursuits are specialized in. This tendency is seen in the attempt which is constantly being made not to regard as secondary education any forms of later education intended for ex-elementary school scholars, so that we have the phrases "night schools," "continuation schools," "higher elementary schools," and "trade schools," springing up and kept outside the conventional and professional view of what secondary education is.

In seeking to evolve any satisfactory system of education, these mistaken and confused conceptions of secondary education must be swept away, and secondary education must be held to embrace all forms of further teaching and training which succeed the training appropriate for lower ages.

The need for greater variety of Secondary Schools.

If we are to have any sort of national system of education, it follows that there must be a great variety in the types of secondary schools which we set up. It is an essential part of the case that is being put forward that elementary education can never be complete in itself, and that every child requires some form of secondary education. But the secondary schools must be sufficiently varied as. to meet the needs of the varying gifts and aptitudes of the children of the nation. If the training of the child in the elementary school has been adequate, it would generally be possible, at least tentatively, to come to some decision as to the kind of further education for which he is best fitted. Hitherto, the curriculum of the secondary school has proceeded along definite academic lines, and has neglected, in a very great degree, manual training. This point is emphasized in the report of the committee on practical work in secondary schools which has just been issued. There must, therefore, not only be a literary type of secondary school, but a great variety of other types, not only giving much more manual training generally, but having also a direct vocational basis, giving at least the foundations of the training appropriate for certain definite work in later life. The few trade schools which exist in London and in one or two other cities are, of course, secondary schools, and must be recognized as definitely within the system.

To what goal should the Secondary Schools lead?

We have endeavoured to show that, like the elementary schools, the secondary schools should be regarded as a link in the chain of the system of national education. What, however, is the stage which follows secondary education? It is not easy to answer such a question in a word. We have appealed for a greater variety in secondary education in order that it may lead to numerous paths of entry into the work of life. In some cases they must prepare for the universities, not only Oxford and Cambridge, but the universities which are now springing up in most of the big cities of the country, and it is to be hoped will be greatly increased in the near future. The secondary school must also prepare boys for entry into foundations for specialized study—like the agricultural colleges. But for the great majority of their boys for many years to come, the secondary schools must so train their pupils as to enable them on leaving immediately to begin with efficiency their career in the work of life. This can only be done by a very great increase in the number of types of schools and in adequate specialization being undertaken in them.

The cost of Secondary Education.

If secondary education is to be made available for the children of the nation generally, it is obvious that far-reaching changes must be made in the cost which at present falls upon the parents. The scholarship system which simply takes a few of the elementary school children is inefficient, and the ultimate solution will be the establishment of free secondary schools. An intermediate step would be to exempt from payment the children of all parents whose income is below a certain amount. Such a method would work automatically, and without it becoming public which children were admitted free. It would also follow a principle already properly embodied in much of recent legislation. Mere freedom from fees would not be sufficient to meet the cases of the extremely poor, for whom maintenance allowances to cover clothing, books and food, would have, in addition, to be made. We discuss elsewhere the question of the share to be borne by the State of the cost of all education.

Examinations.

The multitude of outside examinations is an admitted evil. A central Examinations Board is necessary which should issue certificates certifying the subjects in which the scholar has satisfied the Board in an examination of a non-competitive character from which the elements of chance has been eliminated. An adequate standard of knowledge and attainment must always be required so that the value of the certificate would be indisputable. But the Examination Board must not be confined to the academic type of secondary school, but must be open to the scholars in all types of schools where secondary education is given.

CHAPTER VIII

AN ENQUIRY INTO SECONDARY SCHOOLS, PRIVATE SCHOOLS, ENDOWED EDUCATIONAL CHARITIES AND SPECIAL VOCATIONAL SCHOOLS

The Board of Education has recognized 986 secondary schools as being efficient. There are about 13,000[1] additional secondary schools under private management, and receiving no financial aid from public funds, of which the Board knows nothing. In the organization of our educational system, adequate knowledge of these privately managed schools is necessary. Their numbers, their efficiency, their curricula, are matters of which the State should have full knowledge. And this not for any hostile purpose, for it is surely to be desired that all private work which merits support should receive encouragement, but it must be efficient, and it should take its properly related place in a national system of education.

A Royal Commission on Private Schools.

Such a survey could scarcely be carried out by the ordinary machinery of a Government department. It

[1] This estimate was given by Mr Pease at the Eighty Club, April 4, 1913.

would require the authority of a commission. Such a commission with the expert assistance it would command, need not be very long in reporting. Its terms of reference would naturally include an enquiry into all privately managed schools, their curricula, their efficiency, the numbers of their scholars, together with recommendations showing the place they might take in a national system of education, though without unnecessary interference with their management and methods, and their distinctive work.

But particularly it is necessary to ascertain what endowments are held by these schools for the purpose of education. Accurate information on this point becomes a matter of urgent necessity at a time when the State is proposing to organize a general system of organization, and to reconsider the principles upon which State aid should be given. In chapter ix a proposal is made for the establishment of a permanent financial commission at the Board of Education, and it would be essential for the commission in deciding the needs of every area to have full information respecting the endowments and financial resources of the whole of the schools.

Endowed Educational Charities.

Another subject which urgently calls for enquiry is the endowed charity schools scattered throughout the country. Sometimes these are called Hospitals. They are generally boarding schools taking orphan or destitute children and giving them industrial and other training. There are cases within the knowledge of the writer where admission to these endowed schools is dependent upon the infant candidate being able to recite certain psalms and the catechism. There are others where they are sent automatically to earn their living on reaching the age of 14. There are good reasons for believing that many of these charity schools have not kept abreast with the progressive movement in education, and that ignorance and unwisdom (and sometimes perhaps abuses) have become features of their management. The interests of the nation call for enquiry by the State, and where necessary for action to follow.

The Choir Schools.

Enquiry is also called for into schools founded for what may be described as limited vocational purposes. The chief of these are the choir schools, instituted not to prepare boys for a musical career in later life, but to supply boy choristers for cathedrals, colleges, etc. Sometimes these schools are exclusively schools for choristers who are obliged to leave when their voices break. Such an arrangement is wholly disastrous to the boys concerned and enquiry into choir schools should be directed to ascertaining whether it would be possible for them to be amalgamated with ordinary schools in order to prevent the expulsion of the chorister at the period of the breaking of his voice.

Registration of Schools.

The enquiry into all secondary and private schools should be followed by the registration of all schools

4—2

which the Board of Education consider efficient, whether aided by public funds or not. Only by State registration can the public be protected from the inefficient and worthless, but it is of fundamental importance that the registration shall take place in an enlightened way, that there shall be no attempt to stereotype any pattern of school or to hinder private enterprise and initiative, to which education owes so much, or to discourage variety. Hence I should like to see some kind of appeal allowed to an educational court in the case of schools which were refused registration.

CHAPTER IX

THE FINANCE OF EDUCATION

It is clear that no great progress can be made in the establishment of a national system of education without additional heavy cost being incurred. It is equally clear that it is idle to look to the local authorities to incur additional burdens. To do so would be effectively to kill any chance of that general enthusiasm for education which we desire to see kindled and extended. It is obvious that the new burden must be borne by the State, and that the existing cost which falls upon local authorities must be the matter of examination and adjustment. The House of Commons has definitely accepted this view and in 1910 it passed unanimously a resolution declaring that the national exchequer should bear an increased share of the expense of the national service of education.

The present system is one of grants based upon attendance. The following important points are to be noted in connection with this system :

1. The State at present contributes about £13,000,000 to all forms of education.

2. The share borne by the rates has continually increased. That borne by the State has remained approximately the same.

3. The cost falls with unfair variation upon different localities. Small schools are relatively more expensive than big schools. An area where the population is close together offers fewer difficulties than an area where the population is scattered. It is much more costly in the latter case to provide proper educational facilities.

4. The result has been unequal educational conditions throughout the country, and consequent inefficiency.

5. The provision for all forms of secondary education is generally inadequate throughout the country and the present payments by the State are not sufficient to secure adequate advance by the local authorities.

6. Experimental work, so essential in education, is hampered, and frequently prevented, by lack of funds.

The Federal Council of Secondary Schools Association has prepared a scheme[1] for a new basis of State grants. In view of the support given to this proposal by educational authorities we reproduce extracts showing the chief points of the scheme:

"*The principle hereby advocated is the single one of changing the unit on which State grants are based from the pupil to the teaching staff.* Grants at present are made in respect of attendance of pupils. The change

[1] Issued July 1913.

now suggested is to make grants depend upon salaries of teachers.

"The apportionment of burden between Rates and Taxes would for the first time be based on a principle at once sound, effective and permanent. The change suggested would place the cost of teaching upon the State ; it would leave to Local Authorities and other School Authorities the cost of maintenance (apart from salaries), and of providing buildings and equipment as needs arise ; and it would tend to raise the standard of school efficiency throughout the country. This plan would have the advantage also of focussing attention, for a time at least, on essentials. It seems imperative for the sake of educational progress that *for a few years the efforts for betterment should be concentrated on teaching power*, and that the first place should not as hitherto be held by the less important items of building and equipment.

"It appears from statistics issued by the Board of Education[1] that teachers' salaries, whether in Elementary or Secondary Schools, account for from 70 to 75 per cent. of the total cost of maintenance. It is this item of expenditure which is the most burdensome to Local Authorities, not only because it is already con-

[1] For Elementary Schools, see Statistics of Public Education in England and Wales, 1910–11–12 (Cd 6551), Part II. Financial Statistics, Tables 134 and 146.

For Secondary Schools, see Parliamentary Paper (Cd 5951) presented to the House of Commons in November, 1911 ; and, for all kinds of Grant-earning Institutions, House of Commons Return (No. 115) for the year 1911–12, relating to Education in England and Wales, presented 6 May, 1913.

siderable, and must, if only by automatic increment of salaries, increase from year to year, but also because the advantages accruing from this heavy and increasing expenditure, unlike expenditure on buildings and equipment, cannot readily be evaluated, and consequently fail in most cases to appeal either to electors or to administrative authorities.

"The State at present is contributing for England and Wales for the general purposes of Education about £13,000,000 (Elementary £11,750,000; Secondary £750,000; Technological £500,000). If the State were to make its contribution equivalent in amount to the present expenditure upon teachers' salaries and other emoluments, it is estimated that in the first instance the charge on public funds would amount to about £19,000,000 (Elementary £16,000,000; Secondary £2,000,000; Technological £1,000,000).

"If it be objected that an increase of £6,000,000 at once, with a prospect of a further rise as soon as the new scales come into force, would be too much to ask of the State, it may be answered that the principle of basing grants on salaries would still be asserted if the State were to make grants equivalent to four-fifths or some other preponderating fraction of the cost of salaries.

"Such a revised system of grants would relieve Local Authorities of a burden which admittedly renders their work difficult, and in many cases is making education unpopular with the electorate.

"At present in Elementary Education there appears

to be an increasing shortage, not only in the number of qualified teachers, but also in that of teachers of any kind. Unless, therefore, the attractiveness of posts in these schools can be substantially increased, educational progress must be seriously retarded. In the field of Secondary Education, where the *personnel* of the staff is of vital importance to efficiency, there is so serious a lack of fully qualified teachers as to place England in a position inferior to that of some other countries *in the efficiency of the average Secondary School.*

"Thus both in Secondary and in Elementary Education a new departure directly authorized by Parliament is imperative, if a regular supply of efficient teachers is to be made available throughout the country. Such a departure would not only stimulate and encourage individual teachers but would associate them in corporate service and would lay the basis of an united and efficient professional body.

"With a well-founded expectation of reasonable emoluments, fair prospects and professional status, a larger number of able persons would qualify themselves to become teachers. *Such persons would not become Civil Servants, inasmuch as School Authorities and Local Authorities would continue to appoint, pay, and dismiss their teachers.* A more uniform status would, however, naturally tend to the mobility and interchange of teachers throughout the country and would diminish among them such inequalities as now arise from purely local conditions.

"An important corollary to the new departure is that the State would thus be enabled to take steps to raise the general standard of qualifications required from teachers, and in particular from those in Secondary Schools. At present (except in the case of the Heads of certain schools) no such standard exists, the question of qualifications being left entirely to individual Governing Bodies. In this respect, more than in any other, England is behind other countries, where a high standard of attainment and of ability to teach is secured by Government requirements as to qualifications and training, and is recognized by adequate salary scales.

"*A system of schools thus staffed would bring about to an increasing extent that equalization of school opportunities which must be a main object of educational organization in a democratic State.*

"Such a system would require that, as heretofore, the Board of Education should inspect all grant-earning schools, while Local Authorities should consider the educational needs of their areas, and after consultation with the Board should provide or aid necessary schools and other teaching institutions. To such duties and responsibilities the scheme advocated would add, so far as the Board is concerned, the duty of establishing some classification of schools, and of determining the numbers and qualifications of school staffs together with appropriate salary scales.

"In this connexion it will be obvious that an extension of powers, so as to require inspection, at the cost of the State, of all kinds of schools and teaching institutions, must be authorized by Parliament. Such schools and institutions, if declared efficient within certain ranges of age and work to be specified by the

Board of Education, would be entitled to State recognition within their respective ranges. Without such an extended survey and recognition no truly National System of education can come into existence.

" In short, if a National System is to be established, fresh interest must be aroused in all quarters. Schools must be vitalized; teachers must be welded into a professional body; Local Authorities and School Authorities must be stimulated and aided; while the State itself must definitely assume responsibility for seeing that schools and other teaching institutions are efficient, and that equal educational opportunities are brought within the reach of all who desire to learn."

The scheme here set forth merits and will receive the careful attention of the education department. It is not necessary for the present writer to examine it in further detail, or to submit it as the only or the best solution of the existing difficulty. It is, however, necessary to set forth the principles to be observed in settling the financial basis for a national educational system :

(*a*) The State must bear a far greater proportion of the cost of education.

(*b*) It would be inadvisable to require from the ratepayers a larger contribution per child than they are now paying in progressive and efficient areas.

(*c*) A grant given in the main on the basis of attendance is not satisfactory.

(*d*) The State will properly require every local authority not to fall below a certain minimum contribution per child, but should provide whatever balance is necessary for an efficient system.

(*e*) A special building grant for schools provided by the local authority must accompany any scheme of financial reform. Only in this way can the present evils of overcrowding, and the exclusion of many children, be removed.

(*f*) Financial provision must be made to secure adequate pensions for secondary school teachers.

The result of (*d*) would be that the education rate would practically be equalized throughout the country. Whatever balance was necessary would be supplied from the national exchequer subject to the approval of the Board of Education of the educational plans and work of each local authority.

A Permanent Financial Commission.

This plan would require a revolution in the present methods of the education department, and the writer suggests the establishment as an integral branch of the Board of a permanent financial commission, upon which outside representatives would sit, whose duties would be to examine the schemes necessary for each area, and having considered all relevant facts, decide the amount of the State grant necessary, in order to provide an adequate and coordinated system of education.

CHAPTER X

UNIVERSITY REFORM

No proposals for the reform of our educational system would be complete without reference to the Universities of Oxford and Cambridge. For some years there has been an insistent demand for a Royal Commission of enquiry. That movement has so far failed in achieving its object, but we believe its demand to be just, necessary, and, ultimately, irresistible.

The Case for a Commission.

What is the case for a Royal Commission? It is a vital mistake to think of those who demand a commission as enemies of the universities, or as having any other view than that of enabling them better to fulfil their mission in the national life. The case for a commission is based upon two broad grounds, first, on certain general principles, and secondly, on the necessity for certain specific reforms, believed to be a matter of immediate necessity. That part of the case which rests on general principles may be summarized as follows:

1. The universities are a national institution doing national work. They cannot be divorced from the general educational machinery of the country or remain

rigidly fixed to old methods and machinery, unrelated, or inadequately related, to modern needs.

2. It is not a sufficient reply to the appeal for a commission to urge that the universities are maintained by endowments left by private persons, and that they are for the most part independent of help from outside sources. The universities are indeed the immediate trustees of the benefactions left them for the purposes of higher education. But the ultimate trustees are the State, which alone possesses the power and the disinterestedness to bring co-ordination and unity between independent, and sometimes antagonistic interests, to see that the spirit is not sacrificed to the letter of their trust, and that the general interests of the beneficiaries who are the people of the entire nation, are adequately secured.

3. Nor is it a sufficient reply to urge that the universities are efficiently governed, and should be left to work out their own salvation. Even if there were no obvious anomalies, or challengeable methods, or unwise isolation, or wasteful overlapping calling for alteration and reform, the case for enquiry would remain unweakened. No institution, however glorious, should remain without the stimulus, from time to time, arising from impartial enquiry, criticism, and suggestion. These latter are especially urgent now when we are seeking after a scientifically related system of national education.

On the other side of the case for a commission, the chief specific points towards which reform should be directed are considered under the following heads.

These are intended to be suggestive only, not exhaustive. Of all of them it is probably true to say that the driving power which would come from the recommendations of a Royal Commission is necessary before they can be dealt with.

1. The universities are isolated. In view of the great changes and development proceeding in other fields of education, the place and function of the universities in the educational system generally, call for reconsideration. The State has developed a system of education which touches, and in part regulates, all other phases of education. The old universities proceed on their own way. It may be a good way, yet some divergence from it may be necessary if only that the paths from other fields of education may reach it.

2. The form of government of the universities calls for modification. The power now rests with non-resident electors out of touch with the universities, who frequently prevent even moderate reforms being carried through. This dead hand upon the progress of the universities must be removed, and a form of government which would give the universities the power to adapt their methods to new conditions, unfettered by the veto of absent graduates, is essential. One method of achieving this would be the establishment of a governing council composed of representatives of each college.

3. The establishment of such a governing council would be the first step towards placing adequate financial control in the hands of the universities. At present the constituent colleges control their own income. This

leads to a variety of undesirable results, some of which are as follow:

(*a*) It is a wasteful system. A college is able to make its plans without reference to other colleges and the needs of the university generally. Costly professorships or lectureships may be founded which are unnecessary in view of the work of other colleges, or may be maintained when they have ceased to be required.

(*b*) It is inefficient. It prevents a real synthesis in the work of the university as a whole, since every college is a law to itself.

4. The average cost of residence at the university is too high. The fees should be lowered and it should be generally easier for poor men to enter the universities. There should be a development of the hostel system, and many of the details in connection with the residential side of university life should be simplified and rendered less expensive, whilst being made more efficient.

5. An end should be put to the system whereby scholarships intended to aid poor students are won and held by the sons of wealthy parents. The present system is a serious misuse of the scholarship benefactions. It ought not to be a difficult matter to provide for the automatic working of an income limit above which no scholarship could be held. Such a plan could be accompanied by an arrangement under which a scholarship could be won by anyone irrespective of wealth, but to carry no financial help except for those whose income is under the agreed limit.

6. The privilege of university residence must not be appropriated by men who have no intention seriously to avail themselves of its facilities for study. The universities must be rigorously reserved for students.

7. Adequate use is not made of the universities. The educational capital of our university buildings lies idle for a large part of the year. In the chapter on the higher education of adults, suggestions are made in this connection.

8. The claims of women students have not been adequately recognized, and the disabilities under which they suffer call for removal. This question raises fundamental considerations respecting the conception of the place of a university in the educational life of a nation.

9. The universities and the Board of Education should more closely co-operate in the general field of educational science. Such co-operation would promote the greater efficiency and usefulness alike of the Board and the universities. This closer unity might well begin by a representative of the Board of Education, appointed with the sanction of Parliament, sitting upon the governing body of each university. Such a representative would really be an ambassador between the two educational powers. His mere vote would be almost a negligible quantity, but his presence appears, at least to the writer, to be almost a necessity if efficient co-operation in the organization of the education of the country is to be secured.

CHAPTER XI

THE HIGHER EDUCATION OF THE ADULT CITIZEN

No reform and extension of our national system of education can be satisfactory which does not include the higher education of adult citizens. We must aim at rousing in the country the desire for a fuller life for all citizens, not merely for our growing children. In Denmark where perhaps the level of education is higher than in any other country the people's high schools have been built up on the basis of voluntary private initiative, aided by State grants and bursaries. Can we not aim at some such system here, the Exchequer aiding both local authorities and voluntary associations in the provision of such higher education for working people, both men and women?

The response which these make to the opportunity for higher education has been amply shown in recent years in connection with the success which has attended the university extension, and tutorial movements, and particularly the work of the Workers' Educational Association.

It would be natural to look both to the old and to the new universities to become the chief organizers of further developments in this field of education.

Properly conceived, a university should be much more than an examining or teaching body, or even a residential centre for study and research. A local university should be also the appropriate centre of the intellectual life of the city to which it belongs, working in close co-operation with all the other educational and social forces of the city, and placing all its knowledge and resources and powers of initiative at the disposal of the citizens.

In particular we need to remember that the educational capital of our university buildings lies idle for a large part of the year. We might make the best use of our 18 English universities and university college buildings by holding during the long vacation summer courses for working people, aided by State grants or bursaries. If working people could look forward to going to such a course perhaps once in five years, and then return to their ordinary work, the whole standard of our national life would be raised.

The local University should have regard to local circumstances. It should attempt to give guidance to, and encourage co-operation amongst, all the educational forces around it. In connection with adult education it has now a unique opportunity of supplementing the work of the schools both elementary and secondary. The work of these schools has been in part wasted because it has not received the adequate co-operation of the parents, largely owing to indifference based on ignorance.

It would be appropriate for the University to

secure this co-operation, and by means of lectures, publications and special tutorial classes, enlist the sympathy of parents in the work of the schools and, particularly, to interest them in subjects where their co-operation is essential, e.g. the proper kinds of food for school children, the hours of sleep, hygienic clothing and other matters affecting the health of the child.

The local University should also guide the adult community in its study of the whole problem of Civics.

CHAPTER XII

THE RELIGIOUS QUESTION

The saddest of all aspects of our educational system is that connected with the word "religion." The word education has come to stand in the minds of many for a bitter sectarian wrangle, and it is less than the truth to state that urgent and vital educational reforms have for many years been neglected because of this unhappy controversy. Happily, there are signs that it is coming to an end, but whether this be so or not, there is an increasing volume of informed opinion throughout the country which insists upon placing on one side these religious quarrels and dealing with the real things of education. The Lord Chancellor has recently expressed the hope that the education difficulty will be taken in a stride, and by his words he has probably succeeded in placing the question in its true perspective. It is really a very limited and a very small question, but through the bitterness which it has created it has assumed an importance greater than that to which it is entitled. It is, however, obvious that the State must face the question in its new educational policy.

The main grievance of nonconformists is the single school area. So long as they have no option but to send their children to a school, the religious atmosphere of which is alien to their beliefs, no real peace is possible. However much it is to be regretted that the difficulty should have occupied so large a place in the general educational question, the justice of the claim of the nonconformists can hardly be questioned, and the removal of their undoubted grievance must accompany educational reform. Into the details of this long-discussed question it is not the intention of the writer to go. But the existing difficulty will be substantially solved by placing a State school within the reach of every child, or by enabling every child to reach one.

It is mournful that the struggle between the Church schools and the undenominational schools has sometimes been regarded as a contest between those who desired religion in the schools and those who wished it excluded. It is nothing of the kind, and not the least evil connected with its continuance is that it has tended to prevent us as a nation from considering what are the greatest religious and formative influences which can be given play in our elementary schools.

No wise person desires to see religious influence banished from the schools. No view could be more mischievous than to think of the duty of a school as being first to teach certain subjects which will enable the children who leave them to earn their bread and butter in later years. The first duty of the school is to cultivate and build up noble characters. If the school does not do this it has failed, and no success in teaching vocational subjects will atone for the failure. But, in order to give full play to religious influence, it is not necessary to insist upon the teaching to young children of the dogmatic views of particular schools of theological thought. These are matters of secondary importance. All the great and final things which produce strong and noble character—reverence, truth, courage, gentleness—these are not dependent upon such teaching. Rather, they recede into the background when the less important are unduly pressed forward.

The whole life of the school should be studied and organized to bring these, the best of all religious forces, to bear upon the child. Physical and mental health are to be cultivated in order to produce moral health, and in a very real sense every detail of the school's work is religious and has a religious object. And, so far as the State schools, at least, are concerned, having secured the essential things in life and character, we may leave it for other agencies, at a later stage, to press the distinctive claims of sectarian dogma.

But the greatest of all influences in the schools will be the personality of the teacher. It is he who will write upon the plastic heart and mind, kindle the fire of hero worship, inspire with noble idealism, and guide the unfolding character with all its weakness and immaturity to a full development and the realization of some, at least, of its splendid possibilities.

Let us see to it that the men and the women to whom we entrust the greatest of all tasks are worthy of the trust.

CHAPTER XIII

A JOINT GOVERNMENT BOARD TO DEAL WITH ALL
EDUCATIONAL AND LEGISLATIVE QUESTIONS
AFFECTING THE YOUNG

In the past the organization of education and the
development of legislation designed to protect the
adolescent have been hampered and rendered less
efficient by the fact that the responsibility for various
phases of the life of young persons, so far as it is
touched by legislation, is divided amongst a number
of Government Departments. The Board of Education is concerned with education in its narrower aspect,
namely, as set forth in the various Education Acts.
The Home Office is concerned with the protection
of children and young persons under the Factory Acts,
and other Acts like the Employment of Children Act
of 1903, and is also concerned with the care of children
and young persons detained in various punitive or
semi-punitive institutions, e.g., Borstall, and the Reformatory and Industrial Schools. The Board of
Trade has certain responsibilities in connection with
the young, particularly through the Juvenile Labour
Exchanges. The Local Government Board is responsible for the children in the workhouses and in
the Poor Law Schools.

This division of authority amongst departments having no essential unity has led to much confusion and overlapping in the past. Where legislation has been introduced it has frequently been brought forward from the aspect of one department only, and the problem dealt with has not been surveyed as a whole. In seeking to establish a National System of Education, this question of the responsibility of different Government Departments becomes an urgent one. It has frequently been emphasized by Royal Commissions and Departmental Committees, and many suggestions have been made with a view to removing existing anomalies. The writer suggests that it would be appropriate to regard the Board of Education as the department which should, as far as possible, be entrusted with the enforcement of all legislation concerned with the young, and with the initiation of such legislation. Where initiation took place by other departments it should be in conjunction with the Board of Education. Only in this way will the desired unity be obtained and all legislation affecting the young be considered as a whole and especially in relation to the problem of education in its widest aspects.

We would suggest, as one way of securing the end in view, the establishment of a Joint Government Committee with headquarters at the Board of Education consisting of representatives of all the other departments who are in any way concerned with legislation affecting persons under 21 years of age. This would include the Home Office, the Board of

Trade, the Local Government Board and the Treasury. Such a Committee would discuss and arrange with the Board of Education the details of all legislation to be brought forward and it would be the duty of the Committee, in conjunction with the Board of Education, to see that it harmonized with, and was related to, the general tendency of educational reform.

An immediate question which would arise for the consideration of such a joint Board would be the overlapping which now takes place in the inspections carried on by independent departments of State, and the methods by which this could be reduced without waiting for the complete transfer to the Board of Education of functions now performed by other departments.

CHAPTER XIV

THE POSITION OF POOR LAW SCHOOLS AND IN-
DUSTRIAL AND REFORMATORY SCHOOLS IN A
STATE SYSTEM OF EDUCATION[1]

No survey of a national system of education would
be complete without some reference to the great
numbers of children who are being educated in Poor
Law Schools under the control of Boards of Guardians,
and of the children who are reared in the Industrial
and Reformatory Schools scattered throughout the
country. The case of the children in the Poor Law
Schools was exhaustively considered by the Royal
Commission on the Poor Laws, and there is little to
add to the presentment of the case made in the
Minority Report of the Commissioners, who desire
to see these children removed from the control of
the Poor Law authorities and placed under the Board
of Education. No relevant objection has been advanced against this proposal, and the schools themselves must remain a sort of educational backwater
until this has been done.

[1] The proposals in this chapter respecting Industrial and
Reformatory Schools were made by the author in his capacity as
a member of the Departmental Committee on these schools in a
memorandum which accompanied the Report of the Committee to
the Secretary of State.

The position of the children in the Reformatory and Industrial Schools is a more complicated one. We inherit a system which has grown up slowly as the result of private enterprize. It is one that offers many anomalies : the schools for the most part are under private management, yet the entire cost of the children detained in them is defrayed by the joint contributions of the Imperial Exchequer and local authorities. To these private schools children are committed by magistrates, sometimes for serious offences, but in a great number of cases for trivial offences. The schools do not form part of the educational machinery of the country, and are inspected by the Home Office. For nearly three years a Departmental Committee, appointed by the Home Secretary, has sat, to enquire into the whole question of the management and reform of these schools, and their Report has just been made public. It contains a great number of suggestions on points of detail which are unanimously concurred in, but on the larger question of policy the Report takes the shape of a compromise between those who desire to see the schools handed over entirely to the Board of Education and those who desire to see them controlled as heretofore by the Home Office, and the Committee content themselves with recommending that the educational side of the schools should be inspected by the Board of Education, the Home Office remaining responsible for the inspection of the schools apart from their educational side.

I do not regard the proposed compromise as satisfactory if it is to be a permanent arrangement.

Two vital weaknesses have been revealed in the system of Industrial and Reformatory Schools: (1) the majority of them are under private management, with insufficient funds and resources generally; and (2) they are divorced from the general educational life of the nation.

A gradual evolution has taken place in the conception of the function of Industrial and Reformatory Schools. They were originally regarded in many cases as places of detention and punishment, committal to which was sometimes preceded by a term of detention in an ordinary prison. It is now generally recognized that their function is mainly educational. The character of the children who are committed to these schools has altered since the early years of their establishment. The beginning of this change was noted by the Royal Commissioners so far back as the year 1884. This change is, in my opinion, mainly due to the general progress of social reform and education, which have practically stamped out many of those forms of juvenile crime the authors of which formerly filled these schools. To-day children are committed to many of these schools at a tender age for faults of their parents or guardians, and in many cases the petty offences of which they have been guilty are the results of inadequate parental care and control, and must not be held as permanently distinguishing their youthful authors from children in general.

So long as these schools were regarded as primarily custodial and penal in character it was natural that their supervision should be in the hands of the Depart-

ment of State concerned with the criminal law and that
little attempt should be made to regard these schools
as a local problem of education and training rather
than as a national problem of crime.

The children who are sent to the schools come for
the most part from certain large centres of population.
To take an example, the schools in Manchester, Liverpool, and district contain over 4,000 children, or more
than a quarter of the entire population of these schools
in England and Wales. Not all of these children
come from the cities mentioned, for the schools receive
children from any part of the country, but, on the other
hand, Liverpool and Manchester children are often
sent to schools in other towns or districts.

Owing to the form in which the available statistics
are presented, it is not possible to show the exact
number of children now in the schools who come from
certain big cities. It appears clear, however, that the
majority come from a small number of cities, including
London, Manchester, Liverpool, Birmingham, New-
castle, Bristol, and a few others.

This point is important in connection with any
proposal to place upon Local Education Authorities
the direct responsibility for the schools to which their
children are sent, for it shows that the problem is a
local one, and mainly serious in crowded centres of
population. The problem is in part created by the
social conditions existing in these centres and by the
prevalence of juvenile street trading.

I am of opinion that both the Industrial and
Reformatory Schools should be regarded as a part

of the educational machinery of the country, and that they should be placed, wherever possible, under the local education authorities, subject to the regulations and supervision of the Board of Education in the same way as the whole of the elementary schools and all other schools maintained by local authorities are subject. I recognize that the policy of transferring the schools from private ownership and management to the local authorities throughout the country could not be immediately completed.

A special department for the inspection and supervision of the schools should be formed at the Board of Education. The Board would be responsible for the complete inspection of the schools, and the Treasury contribution would be dependent upon the schools being approved by the Board. It should further be the duty of the Board of Education to arrange as rapidly as may be for the various local education authorities interested to assume the management of the schools and reformatories to which their children are sent. This change should be accomplished with as little interference as possible with the boards of voluntary management which at present control many of the schools, and if the plan is carried out it would result in the following system :—A separate board of managers for each school containing all the efficient members of existing boards of managers, with whatever other members drawn either from their own body or from elsewhere the local education authority care to appoint; above these boards of managers would be the local education authority ; behind the local education authority would be the Board of Education. This system would be analogous to that which exists in the case of both the Elementary and Secondary Schools under, say, the London County Council. The duties of the three bodies would be, roughly, as follows:

The board of managers attached to each school would be responsible for details of administration and the general care and management of each school, as they are now, and would perform whatever other duties were delegated to them by the education authority. The local education authority, working through the managers, would be responsible for the efficiency of the school, the adequacy of the buildings, and the broad principles of the curriculum. The Board of Education would be the inspecting and inspiring force in the background, performing precisely the same functions that it does in respect of the other schools of the country, and showing backward authorities the proper lines of efficient advance.

The principle of placing upon the local education authorities the direct responsibility for the schools can, as already stated, only be realised by stages. But there are many cases in which it could be quickly carried out, and no new schools should be certified except to a local authority. It would be desirable to begin by the transfer to a local authority of inefficient existing schools as an alternative to withdrawing the certificate.

The appointment of the Board of Education as the Central Authority would avoid a system of dual inspection. I do not believe that the life of the child can be cut into two parts, one of which is regarded as educational and the other as non-educational. The Inspectors who are sent to the schools should be men qualified to view the life of the institution as a whole. Moreover, the educational training cannot be divorced from the complete life of the institution, as, e.g., the hours of sleep and play, the diet, the arrangements for washing and for play. And if the department controlling the Industrial and Reformatory Schools remains at the Home Office, it would still be highly desirable, either by using the Board of Education's Inspectorate or by the method of full independent report on each school by the Board of Education at regular intervals, to avoid dual inspection. Such a system appears to me to be wasteful and to rob the Inspectorate of real responsibility and driving power.

In many cases the curriculum of the schoolroom appeared to me to be on very rigid lines and the subjects were not taught in the most interesting way. More experiment in educational methods would be desirable ; particularly far greater use should be made of handwork as a method of instruction within the schoolroom, especially in the case of younger boys. The influence of literature is not sufficiently recognized in some of the schools. No attempt is made, as a rule, to teach hygiene, or even the elementary laws of health, and this might be made a compulsory subject. It would also be desirable to have much more singing and music in the schools, and in this connection I suggest that the band should not be divorced from the ordinary singing practised in the school, but should be used to assist the latter. The provision of a song book containing first class pieces appealing to boys is desirable.

With regard to the industrial training given in practically all the schools, the object aimed at of preparing every boy to earn his living at a trade when he leaves the school is wholly desirable. It is, however, impossible to study the statistics of the disposal of the children leaving the schools without realising that in a great number of cases the industrial training given in the school shops is wasted. Nearly every school has its boot-making shop and its tailors' shop, yet out of 9,106 boys who left the schools in three years only 312 were discovered following either the trade of shoemaker or tailor. One superintendent informed me that he had suppressed the boot-making shop because it was no good as a form of disposal and did not save the school any expense. He could buy the boots cheaper than he could make them, and was, in fact, saving £40 a year by the change. I therefore suggest that it would be desirable to consider the immediate abolition of these two shops in a great number of the schools and the substitution of other forms of industrial training. I would also suggest far closer co-operation between the schools which prepare boys for special callings and the authorities directly concerned. Thus, for example, a school which is training boys for the Navy should arrange its curriculum in consultation with the Board of Admiralty; the War Office should be consulted as to the training of the boys intended for the Army; and a school which specially prepares for the merchant service should work in co-operation with the authorities concerned.

The value of the work of the schools would be greatly increased if less reliance were placed upon machine-like discipline and more importance attached to the development of individuality. It is depressing to see big boys march to the meal table, clasp their hands at the call of a number, begin grace at the call of another, and so on till at the final number they fall upon their food. A far higher standard has been reached when the boys observe the amenities of life without this soulless discipline. The individuality of the boys would be promoted by the encouragement of hobbies as (e.g.) scouting, nature study, the making of things in free time, the keeping of pets. School societies for the encouragement of hobbies, and for reading, debating, and rambles, would be all for good and would tend to develop self-government and responsibility.

The annual report which is issued to the public should contain, in addition to other information of general interest or value, a statement of the number of boys who have left each school during the year, with definite particulars of the occupation to which each has been sent.

CHAPTER XV

CO-ORDINATION OF COMMITTEES OF LOCAL
AUTHORITIES

We have spoken elsewhere of the need of giving the power to make a complete educational system in every area by the local authority or authorities of that area, acting where necessary in co-operation with each other. We desire also to discuss the question of the methods in which the educational committees of local authorities are organized so far as their relation with other committees of the same authority is concerned. It has always seemed to the writer an unfortunate arrangement by which the education committee and the committees regulating such departments of the local authorities' work as parks, libraries and museums, are generally in water-tight compartments, and it is the object of this chapter to plead for a better system of co-ordinating the separate committees of local authorities which have to deal with subjects essentially educational. The case of the typical library committee might be cited as an example of what is meant. The work of the library committee of the average local authority has had little relation to the educational system of the district. Many of the school children no doubt have used the local libraries to borrow works of fiction, but there has been no attempt to make the library a real adjunct of the school.   We hope we are not unduly optimistic in looking forward to a day when each public library will have its scholars' room, with a carefully selected library, and facilities for study under sympathetic guidance.   But short of this, very much may be done if the library and the school co-operate to assist the work of the former.   Particularly we would urge that a system should be organized by local authorities whereby an adequate selection of books should be sent into the schools at regular intervals for the purpose of use in the homes of the school children.   It would be possible in this way to supplement much of the teaching in the schoolroom, and especially to give a teacher of individuality the opportunity of getting his pupils to profit by his advice.

Similarly, the local museums should be regarded largely as an adjunct to the schools.   They are very generally neglected in the daytime, and it would be a stimulating change to the scholars to be taken for an occasional lesson during the week into the museum itself, and to be taught the interest and help that can be derived from its contents.   The same statement applies to the local art galleries.   The first attempt to arouse any feeling for beauty should be associated with an intelligent appeal to great pictures or the reproductions of great pictures, and, wherever available, the art galleries should be freely drawn upon.

It is almost unnecessary to point out how useful co-operation by the parks committee might be.   Not only is there urgent need for more adequate facilities to be provided in the public parks for the children of the schools, but much more use might be made of the facilities the parks offer for the beautification of the schools. Every elementary and secondary school within reach of a public park might surely have the loan of flowering trees and shrubs for the decoration of the schoolrooms, as well as for assistance in nature study. We have only hinted at some of the more obvious possibilities within the power of committees of local authorities, but the realization of these, and of many others, demands an alteration of the present system of working in water-tight compartments. The definite educational function of much of the work of the committees mentioned should be realized, and a sub-committee, representative of the various committees affected, should be formed for the purpose of co-ordinating the educational work of the committees, and of preparing and considering practical schemes of related action.

CHAPTER XVI

THE FUNCTIONS OF THE BOARD OF EDUCATION

In the course of this short work, frequent reference has been made to the Board of Education. We should not like it to be assumed that we look toward a system of education entirely dominated by the Government and damping down local initiative and enthusiasm. On the contrary, we feel that local enthusiasm and responsibility are essential if any real progress is to be made, and though we desire to see the functions of the Board of Education greatly enlarged, this is only in order that it may give adequate assistance in advising and helping the great army of organizers and teachers in the educational world. Nothing would be more unfortunate than that the Board of Education should be regarded simply as a central office to check returns and pay over a grant. The Board should be a great inspiring force, bringing the knowledge which alone it is in a position to obtain to the help of all, and promoting by its sympathy and aid every practical suggestion of advance on sound lines. There are a number of developments which a greater educational policy suggests in connection with the Board of Education :

(1) It is time that the Presidency of the Board was recognized as a post in the Government second to none. At present it is not so regarded. It carries with it a salary of £2,000, as against a salary of £5,000 for the chief Cabinet offices, and it has, in the past, frequently been regarded only as a stepping stone to a higher office. The raising of the status and the salary to that of a first-class office in the Cabinet is an essential initial step.

(2) In the past the Board of Education has not been sufficiently experimental. It might well do more in the way of aiding and initiating schemes for pioneer work. To do this it would be necessary to have a larger amount of money available for the purpose of experimental work. It would then be possible for the Board to approach a suitable local authority and get them to undertake such experiments, giving them, of course, an outlined or detailed scheme. In this way developments in foreign countries which have been proved successful might more quickly be brought to the notice of the educational world here, and their value, or otherwise, demonstrated.

(3) The Department of special enquiries and reports at the Board has behind it a record of work done of which it might well be proud. The writer has no sort of criticism to make on it, but would enter an earnest plea for its extension. Particularly, it should issue more frequently publications dealing with experiments in this country, and should, whenever possible, suggest new schemes which might be undertaken by local authorities or others. The average

over-worked teacher has not many opportunities for mixing in a larger world outside his own immediate interests, and could be stimulated and encouraged in many ways by the publications of the Board. Equally helpful would such guidance be to the members of educational authorities.

(4) Much more guidance should be given by the Board in the planning of new schools and in the alterations and improvement to existing ones. An excellent development of the work of the Home Office which is now taking place consists of the establishment of an industrial museum illustrating the solution of problems affecting industrial and other matters supervised by the Home Office. Similarly, the Board of Education might well institute a museum of plans and models, but particularly of models, which should be all kept up to date, and should illustrate, in the best possible way, the most healthy and scientific building and planning of schools and school grounds.

(5) There is great need for research work on definite questions to be undertaken by the Board, or commissioned by the Board. We are behind some other countries in original research, and lack scientific conclusions based upon investigation on some of the most important questions affecting the young[1].

---

[1] As these lines were passing through the press Dr Kimmins submitted a plan to the British Association for research on the following points.—(1) The age at which a child should commence to read and write. (2) The best method of teaching reading. (3) The number of hours a child can profitably spend in school at a given age. (4) The most suitable length of lessons for children

(6) Any study of possible developments in English education shows how many and varied are the functions which the Board of Education may be called upon to discharge. The enlargement of the Board becomes a matter of urgent necessity and its division into more specialized departments. It follows that admittance to the staff of the Board must not be wholly dependent upon competitive examination but must also depend upon the educational and other experiences of the candidate.

(7) The Board (following the example set by the appointment of the Consultative Committee) should more generally use the services of experts outside the Board for advice and guidance on special questions and should associate these with permanent committees.

(8) A permanent financial commission to be established as suggested in Chaper ix. This commission should include representatives of Education, University, Secondary and Elementary, outside the Board.

at different ages. (5) The most satisfactory tests of intelligence. (6) The effect of handwork on other branches of instruction and on general mental efficiency. (7) The varying attitude of children towards certain subjects at different ages. (8) The advisibility of intensive work at certain stages. (9) The extent to which clever children mature late. (10) The degree to which the curricula of girls' should differ from those of boys' schools. (11) The relative amounts of fatigue experienced in learning certain subjects at different ages.

INDEX